Lifted Over The Devil in VICTORY

Samuel Jimson Olorunfemi

Author of Fast Selling Books: ***Quiet Time; Prayer Compass For Victory, Victory in Your Zero Hour*** *and* ***Supernatural Weapons For Believers' Deliverance***

Published by

God's Triumphant Faith Publications,
God's Greatness Plaza,
Behind His Grace Shopping Complex,
Opp. Woleysam Filling Station,
Olorunda Abaa,
After Akobo-Ojurin Ibadan,
Oyo State, Nigeria, West Africa.
Email:sajorev7@yahoo.com
📖 +234 8035624406, +2348055301639, + 2348066371796

ISBN: 979-8846439092

Unless otherwise indicated, scriptural quotations are from the King James Version of the Bible.

Dedication

Dedicated to the Living acknowlegement of God's greatness and His mighty interventions in diverse situations of mine, in life and in ministry, against the opposing forces of darkness and wickedness which result in my constant victory, empowerment, blessing, lifting and progressive movement in fulfilling my mandate on earth. To Him be ascribed all the praise, honour and adoration forever and ever.

Preface

This God's Pen-Weapon, tagged: **"Lifted over the Devil in Victory"** is aimed at opening the eyes of understanding of every true son and daughter of God to His glorious placement for them, at His right hand with Christ Jesus in heavenly places, far above the Devil, all principalities, powers, might and names, mentioned in this age and in ages to come with a view to making them maintain their supreme position of victory over the Devil through Christ Jesus, while on this earth that is full of the wicked and their wicked acts (Col. 1:12-14; Eph. 2:1, 5-7; 1:17-22; Psm. 74:20).

Also elucidated in this "nugget" is the reality of your rescue or deliverance as God's child from being under the influence and control of the powers of darkness and the fact that you have been translated into the kingdom of God's dear Son. (Col. 1:13)

> ***Giving thanks unto the Father, who has made us qualify to be partakers of the inheritance of the saints in the light; Who has delivered us from the power of darkness, and has translated us into the kingdom of his dear son (the son of his love).*** **(Col. 1:12,13)**

Nevertheless, the victory of our Lord Jesus Christ over the Devil and his hosts of darkness on your behalf, your position in triumph over the evil forces, the weapons of war required, the armoury available for you; and the place of the Holy Spirit and His working in you, through you and for you to live and operate in the reality of the triumph are simplified by this work.

Conclusively, you will by this nugget live above the Devil in absolute triumph and God alone will be glorified in your life. Therefore, I commend you to God and to the word of His grace as revelatory made simple by this piece of kingdom's work for you to live in total victory and in glory that will give God the ultimate glory. Surely, your life shall henceforth be that of: victory as against defeat, success as against failure, blessing as against curses, fruitfulness as against barrenness, honour as against dishonour, glory as against shame and reproach, hope as against hopelessness, boldness as against lethargy or fear in Jesus Mighty Name. (Amen).

Rev. Samuel Jimson Olorunfemi Esq.
08035624406
Sajorev7@yahoo.com

Contents

CHAPTER 1

Your Placement Above the Devil in Victory

May I start this page without mincing word that God the Almighty, through Jesus Christ, by His redemptive work at Calvary, that is, His death, resurrection and ascension has quickened and lifted you and I up as His children; and made us to sit together with Him in heavenly places in Christ Jesus!

> ***And you hath he quickened, who were dead in trespasses and sins And hath raised us up together, and made us sit together in heavenly places in Christ Jesus.*** **(Eph.2:1, 6)**

Beloved, while Jesus Christ was crucified at Calvary, you and I were crucified with Him; when He died, we were dead with Him; when He resurrected, we were resurrected with Him; and when He ascended to heaven, we ascended with Him. This is the implication of the crucifixion, death, resurrection and ascension of our Master and Saviour Jesus Christ. This truth is what we have responsibility to reckon ourselves with and appropriate as God's people in order for us to live a life of absolute victory as believers.

In a nutshell, God has made you and I as His children to individually and collectively sit together in heavenly places in Christ Jesus, far above the Devil and all his hosts of darkness.

> ***Far above all principality and power and might, and dominion, and every name that is named, not only in this world, but also in that which is to come.*** **(Eph. 1:21)**

This privilege, right and placement of God for you as His son or daughter far above all principalities and power, and might and dominion and every name that is named in this world and in the ages to come were done in Christ Jesus.

> ***Which he (God) wrought in Christ, when he raised him from the dead, and set him at his own right hand in heavenly places.* (Eph. 1:20)**

Beloved, by this God's act through our Lord and Saviour Jesus Christ, you have been made to sit together at the right hand of God in heavenly places, in victory over and far above the Devil and all His cohorts; and known names in this contemporary world and in that which is to come.

In other words, Devil and his hosts of darkness are down, under you, while you are far above them in victory. This is the truth of God's word which you must accept and imbibe for you to operate in victory over the Devil always in Christ Jesus.

> ***Now thanks be unto God which always causeth us to triumph in Christ and Maketh manifest the savour of his knowledge by us in every place.* (2 Cor. 2:14)**

Amplified version of the bible put the passage above thus:

> ***But thanks be to God, who in Christ always leads us in triumph - as trophies of Christ's victory - and through us spreads and makes evident the fragrance of the knowledge of God everywhere.***

Isn't it marvellous that by the placement of God for your life through Christ, you are not only meant for victory always, but also to be a testifier, a witness and heralder or communicator of what it takes to live and operate in victory to other people? Beloved, you are a follower of Christ in victory as well as a show-piece, proof and emblem of this true victory and you are also saddled with a responsibility to lead others in the knowledge of that victory. Glory! Hallelujah!!

CHAPTER 2

God's Accomplished Work for Your Victory

> ***12 Giving thanks unto the Father, which hath made us meet to be partakers of the inheritance of the saints in light.***
>
> ***13 Who hath delivered us from the power of darkness, and hath translated us into the kingdom of his dear son.*** **(Col. 1:12-13)**

Beloved, God, our Father had made it happen for you and I to be partakers of the inheritance of the Saints – godly people in light as against darkness. The inheritance is that, God first delivered or rescued us from the power of darkness where we were under and at the mercy of the power of darkness while we were not born again; and had translated us into the Kingdom of His dear Son, far above all principality, power, dominion and every host of darkness, when we have become born again.

In essence, you as a son or daughter of God had been delivered from the powers of darkness. You are no longer under the bondage or influence of the powers of darkness. You have been rescued and liberated from them. Thereafter, God removed you from the floor where you were, under the Devil, principalities and every host of darkness, and transferred or lifted you by the force of heaven, far above power of darkness, the fallen Angels and holy Angels, into the highest realm – the kingdom of the dear Son of God – Jesus Christ, where you are seated together in heavenly places in Christ Jesus, at the right hand of God the Father –Glory! (Col. 1:13; Eph. 2:6; 1:21-22).

The following diagram gives illustrative expression of man's translation from power of darkness to the kingdom of God's dear son.

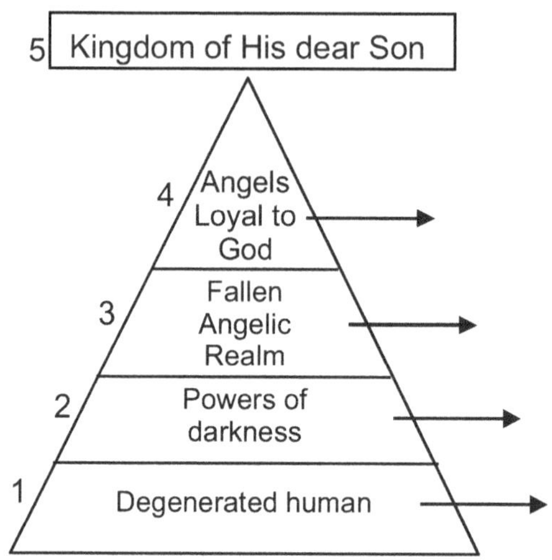

No.1 represents the position of humans when they are not born again. Being at the lowest ebb, directly under the powers of darkness. After being born again, they are translated from that realm to the highest realm, that is, the Kingdom of His dear Son.

No. 2 represents the realm of powers of darkness, still above the realm of human that are not regenerated. The born again human who have been translated from the lowest realm are lifted above that realm.

No. 3 represents the realm of fallen Angels – Satan and all the Angels that were loyal to him who fell with him. The born again humans are lifted up far above that realm from the lowest realm that they were before they got born again.

No.4 represents the realm of God's Angelic beings, whom God had made to be Ministering Spirits to humans who are born again. The regenerated humans have been also translated far above that realm to the highest realm – kingdom of this dear son.

No.5 represents the highest realm – the Kingdom of God's dear Son, where the regenerated humans have been made to sit with Jesus Christ, at the right hand of God the Father. This is the realm that you and I as God's people belong and are translated to from the very day we submit to the Lordship of Jesus Christ.

CHAPTER 3

Reason for Your Lifting Above the Devil in Victory

> ***And hath raised us up together, and made us sit together in heavenly places in Christ. That in the ages to come he might show the exceeding riches of his grace in his kindness toward us through Christ Jesus.*** **(Eph. 2:6, 7)**

The purpose for which God lifted you above the Devil and His cohorts in victory is that: He – God might show the exceeding riches of His grace in His kindness towards us, through Christ Jesus, in this end time. The implication is that God's grace by which we are saved has exceeding riches. These exceeding riches are what God in His kindness wants to make manifest to us. Hence the lifting.

The exceeding riches of God's grace which are for our possession are called **"riches of the glory of his inheritance in the saints"** in the book of Ephesians Chapter 1 and verse 18c

> ***. . . that ye may know what the riches of the glory of his inheritance in the saints.***

Beloved, you are an epitome of the glorious riches of God's inheritance in the saints. You are a vessel that God wants to package the riches of the glory of His inheritance on the inside. Hence He settled everything for your victory over the Devil, so that you can freely possess the glorious riches and victoriously manifest them to His glory. These glorious riches of God's inheritance are highlighted in the Revelation of John, the beloved, Chapter 5 and verse 12 thus:

> ***Saying with a loud voice, worthy is the Lamb that was slain to receive power, and riches, and wisdom, and strength, and honour, and glory, and blessing.***

These glorious riches are interchangeably called the seven redemptive treasures or packages. They are:

1. Power
2. Riches
3. Wisdom
4. Strength
5. Honour
6. Glory and
7. Blessing

All the enumerated above glorious riches are what God wants to open our eyes of understanding to, with a view for us to partake of each of them and enjoy them without hitch or interference from the Devil and his hosts of darkness. Hence, He settled everything about the Devil's defeat on our behalf. Yes, God had defeated Devil on your behalf and on my behalf. Halleluyah!

CHAPTER 4

Jesus' Victory on Your Behalf

> ***And having spoiled principalities and powers, he made a shew of them openly, triumphing over them in it.*** **(Col. 2:15)**

Our Lord Jesus Christ by His redemptive work at Calvary spoilt principalities and powers. He spoilt the Devil and his hosts of darkness and made a public show of their defeat, triumphing over them on your behalf and on my behalf. Beloved, Jesus Christ had triumphed over the Devil and powers of darkness on your behalf. He had cut off their power from your life. What you need to do therefore is to operate and manifest the victory that had already been won for you in Christ Jesus, by studying the word, meditating in it, garnering faith into your heart by the word and acting the word, which is faith in action.

A New Translation James Moffat Bible put our scripture above thus:

> ***. . . he cut away the Angelic Rulers and Powers from us, exposing them to the entire world and triumphing over them in the cross.***

Jesus Christ had defeated Devil on your behalf. What had been defeated on your behalf, do you need to fight to defeat such again? The response is capital 'No'. Therefore, you don't need to war against the Devil any longer. All you need to do therefore is to demonstrate your victory over him as revealed to you in the scriptures (John 8:32), such as: stopping his operations, resisting him, binding him etc in the name of Jesus Christ (James 4:7; Matthew 18:18; 1 Peter 5:8, 9).

Jesus indeed overcame the Devil on your behalf, in order for you to stand tall in victory over him and maintain the victory at all times and in all situations. Hear our Master's declaration of His victory over the Devil and Death:

> ***I am he that liveth and was dead and behold, I am alive for evermore. Amen; and have the keys of hell and of death.*** **(Rev. 1:18)**

The keys of hell and of death are in the hands of Jesus. This is the reason eternal life is given unto you. By the keys in His possession, you as God's son and daughter shall not die untimely and eternally. Glory! Halleluyah! By that possession of the keys of hell and death by the Lord Jesus Christ, God will not leave your soul in hell, neither shall He allow you as His bonafide son or daughter to suffer corruption (being destroyed). Yes! Hell and everything that originate from there have been put under you by the Lord Jesus Christ. It was this revelation that David the king had which made him write and said:

> ***For thou will not leave my soul in hell, neither will thou suffer thine Holy one to see corruption.*** **(Ps 16:10)**

This victory through Christ Jesus was what David the king foresaw that made him set the Lord before himself always, and maintained His presence which he was conscious of. This made him to have a gladden heart, rejoicing in glory and his body had rest in hope as he clearly declared as follows:

> ***I have set the LORD always before me; because he is at my right hand I shall not be moved.***
>
> ***Therefore my heart is glad and my glory rejoiceth; my flesh also shall rest in hope.***

For thou will not leave my soul in hell; neither will thou suffer thine Holy one to see corruption. **(Ps 16:8-10)**

Beloved, Jesus overcame hell and death for your sake and suffered no corruption. Therefore, hell and death are defeated in your life and you shall not suffer corruption. God had settled all these for you in Christ Jesus. Hence the need for you to set before you the Lord Jesus Christ via His word of victory which you should make your focus always. Be conscious of His victory which He had won on your behalf always by heart-faith, based on the word. When you do this, you will not have anything to fear about the Devil or waste your precious time about him. Rather, you will place him in his defeated position, demonstrating your victory over him. Glory to God!

CHAPTER 5

Requirements to Demonstrate Your Victory

1) YOU MUST BE BORN AGAIN

The victory of Jesus Christ over the Devil is for and on behalf of everyone who is born again, by simply acknowledging your sins and acknowledge the fact that you cannot save yourself. Also, you must believe that Jesus Christ came for your salvation, being made a propitiation for your sin. As such, you should ask Him to forgive you your sins and invite Him into your life as your Lord and personal saviour (John 3:3-6; 1:12-13; Rom. 10:8-10, Rev. 3:20). Beloved, it is when you have been saved by the Lord Jesus Christ that you can demonstrate His victory over the Devil always.

> ***Now thank be unto God, which always Causeth us to triumph in Christ, and make manifest the savour of his knowledge by us in every place.*** **(2 Cor. 2:14)**

2) KNOWLEDGE OF THE TRUTH ABOUT YOUR VICTORY

You must have your spiritual eyes enlightened and come to the knowledge of the truth concerning your victory over the Devil. Yes, you must accept this truth about yourself that you have overcome the Devil through Jesus Christ.

> ***You will know the truth and the truth shall make you free.*** **(John 8:32)**

You need to say the same prayer as said by Paul the Apostle in Ephesians, Chapter 1 and verses 17 and 18 thus:

That the God of our Lord Jesus Christ, the Father of glory may give unto you (instead of you, use my and put your name), the spirit of wisdom and revelation in the knowledge of him: The eyes of your (my instead of your) understanding being enlightened that ye (I) may know what is the hope of his calling, and what the riches of the glory of his inheritance in the saints,

This immediate above prayer is paramount with conscientious study of the word of God and absolute reliance on the Holy Spirit to elucidate or simplify the scriptures to you by insight. When the spirit behind the written word, that is, the **Rhema** behind the **Logos** is unveiled to you on any particular word, faith by the word will automatically garner in your heart and the word will become productive to you. The more of the truth of God's word that is revealed to you, the more you will walk and operate in the reality of victory over the Devil.

Beloved, it is through the knowledge of the word of God that you can stand your ground in victory against the Devil. And by it can you enjoy the fullness of the blessings from God's store house that are meant for the saints, amongst whom you are one.

And by knowledge shall the chambers be filled with all precious and pleasant riches. **(Prov. 24:4)**

The word 'chambers' used in the passage above means the innermost being of a person, that is, your real man. Knowledge of God's word will make your life to be saturated with all precious and pleasant riches. James Moffatt Bible says:

And knowledge furnishes the rooms with all that is rare and pleasant.

The importance of knowledge cannot be over estimated or emphasised, just like the woe and misery of ignorance cannot be under estimated.

Beloved, Knowledge also enables a man who is possessed by it to increase in strength, to stand strong in faith and put the Devil on his heels.

. . . A man of knowledge increaseth strength. (Prov 24:5)

3) WISDOM

Wisdom is described as judicious or prudent application of knowledge and Bible calls it the principal virtue that we must ask and seek to possess. With wisdom, you will be in position to judiciously make use of the knowledge of your victory over the Devil to circumvent him, frustrate his plans and stop his operations at every point in time. It is by wisdom you will or can build up yourself in constant victory, and by it you shall be strong.

Through wisdom is a house built. (Prov. 24:3)

. . . for ye are the temple, abode, house or living place of the living God; as God hath said, I will dwelt in them (him), and walk in them (him) shall be their (his) God and they (he) shall be my people (person). (2 Cor. 6:16)

A wise man is strong. (Prov. 24:5)

Wisdom is the principal thing, therefore, get wisdom . . . (Prov. 4:7)

Beloved, wisdom is of God and He is the only entity who can give you the wisdom that you need to maintain and demonstrate your victory over the Devil and all the powers of darkness. You can therefore ask God for the wisdom and you shall receive it.

If any of you lack wisdom, let him ask of God, that giveth to all men liberally, and upbraideth not; and it shall be given him. (James 1:5)

You can also get wisdom by searching, studying, meditating and acting the word of God. Jesus Christ our Lord is wisdom personified and He is the word of God. The more of God's word on your inside determines the measure of God's wisdom on your inside.

> ***In the beginning was the Word, and the Word was with God and the Word was God. The same was in the beginning with God. All things were made by him; and without him was not anything made that was made. And the Word was made flesh, and dwelt among us, (and we beheld his glory, the glory as of the only begotten of the Father) full of glory.*** **(John 1:1-3, 14)**

> ***. . . Christ Jesus, who of God is made unto us wisdom . . . .*** **(1 Cor. 1:30)**

4) UNDERSTANDING

The word "Understanding" literally means 'to perceive the meaning or the nature or the importance of something. It also means 'the act or power of perceiving the truth and making judgments'.

Understanding of knowledge of the truth of God's word concerning the victorious work of Jesus Christ over Satan and how you can reckon with it, and appropriate it in your life will go a long way to enhance the maintenance of the reality of your victorious lifting over the Devil on earth. By understanding, you will be established in victory. What scares others will not scare you. Your faith in God based on His word will be so strong that you will become unmovable. By this, you will stand so strong in the faith to push the Devil off his guards always.

> ***By understanding, the house that you are is established.*** **(Prov. 24:3)**

With the understanding above, you should never get to any level in your life where you become complacent or think that you have arrived on your knowledge and understanding of God's word concerning any issue. The more of understanding of God's word that you have, the more you will need to acquire and have. As you search the scriptures unabatedly, more light of understanding shall be shown into your heart and as you dig deeper into the dip, the deeper shall you be in understanding of each particular subject or issue in God's word and on this subject of your victory over the Devil through Christ Jesus. And take note of the fact that there is no end to understanding of the truth of God's word, because God's ways are past finding.

You can only get this done by maintaining a willing heart to studying, searching, meditating and practising the word of God. 2Tim. 2:15; 3:16; John 5:39; Joshua 1:8; James 1:22-25

> ***Whom shall he teach knowledge? And whom shall he make to understand doctrine? Them that are weaned from the milk, and drawn from the breast. For precept must be upon precept, precept upon precept; line upon line; here a little and there a little.*** **(Isaiah 28:9-10)**

> ***Search the scriptures; for in them ye have eternal life: and they are which testify of me.*** **(John. 5:39)**

Beloved, there is no end to understanding. The day a man stops to learn, that day, he begins to die. Therefore, I commit you to God and to the word of His grace which is able to build you up and give you an inheritance amongst those who are sanctified.

CHAPTER 6

Faith in God's Accomplished Victory

Faith in God's victory which He accomplished on your behalf through Christ Jesus as revealed in His word is what guarantees your maintenance of being lifted over the Devil in victory.

The faith that we are talking about here is triumphant faith. It is a living faith that comes by the living word of God into the heart of a believer. It is a heart-faith as against head and blind faith. It is faith in God that is garnered by personal relationship with Him through His word which we receive into our heart.

> ***Acquaint now thyself with him (God), and be at peace, thereby good shall come unto you. Receive, I pray thee, the law from his mouth and lay up his words in thine heart.* (Job 22:21-22)**

> ***For unto us was the gospel preached, as well as unto them; but the word preached did not profit them, not being mixed with faith in them that heard it.* (Heb.4:2)**

It is when the word of God has had its root in the heart of a believer that faith can be said to have come by the word into that believer. Hence the Almighty God instructionally said:

> ***My son, attend to my words, incline thine ear unto my sayings. Let them not depart from thine eyes; keep them in the midst of your heart.* (Prov. 4:20, 21)**

Beloved, it is when the word of God has had its root in your life (heart) that it can be said that you have found the word. It will then become a victorious life and health to all areas of your life.

> ***For they are life unto those that find them and health to all their flesh.* (Prov. 4:22)**

Reader, your **heart** is the **security organ** of **your life**. That is the reason you are commanded by God and you should have it as your responsibility to guard it jealously. The importance of human heart in the natural is never to be undermined, because it is the living organ in man. The moment the heart beat of man fails, it means that the end of that man has come. Hence it is written:

> ***Keep thine heart with all diligence, for out of it are the issues of life.* (Prov. 4:14)**

The above are the reasons why faith must be of the heart; otherwise, it will not be the kind of faith that God requires from us, which guarantees victory.

In a nutshell, faith is the spiritual force that you must possess that guarantees victory.

Hence it is written that:

> ***. . . whosoever is born of God overcomes the world, and this the victory that overcomes the world, even our faith.* (1 John 5:4)**

Beloved, your own personal faith in God through the accomplished victory of Jesus Christ over the Devil is what guarantees your victorious stance over the Devil. The key factors here are: your faith and our Lord Jesus Christ. Yes! Faith in Him and in His name is what guarantees your victory. Halleluyah!

> ***Who is he that overcometh the world, but he that believeth that Jesus is the son of God? (1 John 5:5)***

> *For whatsoever is born of God overcometh the world and this is the victory that overcometh the world, even our faith (1 John 5:4)*

Hence it is written:

> *Now the just shall live by faith: but if any man draws back my soul shall have no pleasure in him.* (Heb. 10:38)
>
> *For we who have believed do enter into rest, as he said....* (Heb. 4:3)

It is only those who hold unto faith, believing that shall have rest in the finished victorious work of our Lord Jesus Christ in this wicked world that is full of habitation of cruelty.

Beloved, the question that briskly arises here is, do you desire complete rest in the finished victorious works of our Lord Jesus on the cross at Calvary and want to live in demonstration of its reality on earth? If your response is in the affirmative, what you need is *undaunted faith* in God based upon the victory of Jesus Christ. I therefore declare that you shall live the rest of your life in victory in the mighty name of Jesus Christ. Amen.

CHAPTER 7

Reckoning with the Name of Jesus Christ

Our Lord Jesus Christ is the pivot or centre of our victory over the Devil. As such, it is only faith exercised through His name that can make us continue to maintain our victory over the Devil and over powers of darkness. It is only by Him, Jesus Christ and faith in His name that guarantees ceaseless victory for us. I mean victory always. This is the understanding that Paul the Apostle had when He said concerning you and I that:

> ***Now, thanks be unto God, which always Causeth us to triumph in Christ, and Maketh manifest the savour of his knowledge by us in every place.*** **(2 Cor. 2:14)**

Our God is so awesome to us that you and I are guaranteed victory always in Christ Jesus and makes us to manifest the knowledge of the reality of the victory in every place. In other words, apart from the fact that victory is ours always, not some times or for a while, but always in Christ Jesus, it is an "**always victory**," He also makes us a **show-piece**, a living testimony of the knowledge of the victory in every place. Glory!

James Moffatt Bible put the passage above thus:

> ***Wherever I go, thank God, he makes my life a constant pageant of triumph in Christ; diffusing the perfume of his knowledge every-where by me.***

Our Lord Jesus Christ overcame the Devil at Calvary and said ***"it is finished"*** **(John 19:30).** Your defeat has ended, your being under the influence, bondage and at the mercy of the Devil and powers of darkness has finished. Rather, you have been rescued or delivered and transferred from under the powers of darkness into the kingdom of the dear Son of God – Jesus Christ, far above all principality, powers, dominions and names in the now and in the ages to come (Col. 1:13; Eph. 1:21). This same Jesus had God put all things under His feet, and gave Him to be the head over all things to the Church, which is His body, the fullness of him that filleth all in all (Eph. 1:22-23).

After Peter and John had healed the man who had been lame from his mother's womb in the hour of prayer at the gate of the temple which is called Beautiful and there was a pandemonium, as people ran together unto them. Among Peter's words of explanation was:

> ***And his name through faith in his name hath made this man strong; whom ye see and know: yea, the faith which is by him hath given him this perfect soundness in the presence of you all" (Acts 3:16).***

Faith in the name of Jesus is the key to miracles and victory.

(a) THE POWER IN THE NAME OF JESUS CHRIST

> ***Let this mind be in you, which was also in Christ Jesus; Who, being in the form of God, thought it not robbery to be equal with God: But made himself of no reputation, and took upon him the form of a servant, and was made in the likeness of man: And being found in fashion as a man, he humbled himself and became obedient unto death, even the death of the cross.*** **(Phil. 2:5-8)**

Dear beloved, Jesus Christ paid an unprecedented price which none had paid before Him and which no one shall be able to pay thereafter, for Him to earn His powerful name. The price was the price of **humility** and **obedience** to God unto death, even the death of the cross. Hence the anxiom that without a price, there cannot be a glory. Every glory is preceded by a price. The glorious result of our Lord and Master's sacrificial price is as follows:

> ***Wherefore, God also hath highly exalted him, and given him a name which is above every name: That at the name of Jesus, every knee should bow, of things in heaven, and things in earth, and things under the earth. And that every tongue should confess that Jesus Christ is Lord, to the glory of God the Father.*** **(Phil 2:9-11)**

God had highly exalted our Lord and Master Jesus Christ and had given Him a name that is above every name. By that name – Jesus Christ, every knee must bow as well as the knee of everything in heaven, on earth and under the earth and He's so empowered alongside with His name that every tongue shall inevitably confess that Jesus Christ is LORD, to the glory of God the Father. Hallelu-u-yah!

Beloved, there is no other way or other name by which we can enforce Jesus' victory over the Devil except by making use of the name of Jesus Christ. Devil isn't afraid of noise; he doesn't bow to loudness of a person's voice or yelling. He only fears the believer who stands in his authority in Christ.

It is worthy of note to express that the devil doesn't have to cease and desist in his operations against you based on how loud you can yell at him. But he does have to stop in every strategy against you when you exercise your authority in Christ.

Reader, you just have to know your rights and privileges in Christ and enforce Jesus' victory over Satan with God's word. We are not trying to win the victory over Satan. Jesus has already won that victory. We are simply enforcing Jesus' victory with the Word of God in our lives for our advantage and benefits.

(b) THE NAME TO CAST OUT DEMONS AND FOR MIRACLES

Our Lord Jesus Christ said to the Disciples while on earth, before His ascension that:

> ***. . . these signs shall follow them that believe; In my name shall they cast out devils; And they went forth, and preached every where, the Lord working with them, and confirming the word with signs following Amen.*** **(Mark 16:17, 20)**

Our Lord gave us His name to cast out devils. The implication is that, it is only in the name of Jesus that we can cast out devils.

Nevertheless, the Disciples in compliance to the Master's instruction to go and preach the gospel went out and preached everywhere. The result was that the Lord was working with them, and confirming the word with signs following. When you make use of the name, Devil flees, and when you preach the word, which is still Jesus Christ, wonders happen. The name and the word are **catalysts** that cause **catastrophe** to the Devil and the Kingdom of darkness. The word of God is light, while anything that is of the Devil and his hosts represent darkness. When the word of God is preached anywhere, the Devil and his Agents are bound to be dispelled.

> ***Then spoke Jesus again unto them, saying, I am the light of the World; he that followed me shall not walk in darkness, but shall have the light of life.*** **(John 8:12)**

> ***And the light shineth in darkness; and the darkness comprehended it not.*** **(John 1:5)**

A-40 YEAR OLD LAMED HEALED BY THE NAME

A certain man lame from his mother's womb whom they laid daily at the gate of the temple called beautiful gate was carried to the spot at the nineth hour of prayer one day, and on sighting Peter and John who went together to the temple, he asked them for alms. The response that he received was:

> ***Then Peter said, silver and gold have I none; but such as I have give I thee: In the name of Jesus Christ of Nazareth rise up and walk.*** **(Acts 3:6)**

And after the man was healed and crowd gathered in amazement, amongst the words used to testify to the efficacy of the name of Jesus to the people was:

> ***And his name through faith in his name hath made this man strong, whom ye see and know; yea, the faith which is by him hath given him this perfect soundness in the presence of you all.*** **(Acts 3:16)**

Beloved, faith in the name of Jesus Christ guarantees victory, deliverance, miracles, healing and blessings. It is only by that name you can be delivered or deliver anyone from the affliction, oppression, obsession and possession of the Devil.

(c) THE NAME FOR SALVATION

> ***Neither is there salvation in any other: for there is none other name under heaven given among men, whereby we must be saved.*** **(Acts 4:12)**

The power in the name of Jesus Christ is efficacious also in salvation. In fact, no other name under heaven is given among men for salvation, except the name of Jesus Christ.

In fact, it is written that calling upon the name by anyone effects salvation.

> ***For whosoever shall call upon the name of the LORD shall be saved.*** **(Rom. 10:13)**

Also, it is written in the Book of Isaiah, Chapter 45 and verse 22 thus:

"Look unto me, and be ye saved, all the ends of the earth: For I am God and there is none else.

Beloved, faith in the name of Jesus and calling upon the name saves anyone from bondage of sin and eternal destruction and transforms such a person unto righteous-ness and eternal life with Christ.

(d) THE NAME AS A STRONG TOWER FOR SAFETY

The name of the LORD is a strong tower; the righteous runneth into it, and is safe. (Prov. 18:10)

James Moffat Edition of the New Translation Bible puts the passage thus:

The Eternal is a tower of strength: good men run in and are secured.

Beloved, the name of the Lord Jesus is the covering and built-up fortification of strength which guarantees the security of any believer – the righteous, who runs into it, from the reach of the Devil and his hosts of darkness. Halleluyah!

(e) THE NAME OF THE LORD IS A DEFENDER

The LORD hear thee in the day of trouble; the name of God of Jacob defend thee. (Psalm 20:1)

The name of the Lord is a defence and a defender. Beloved, if everyone doesn't have a backing, it does not include you, your backing is Jesus Christ and your defence is His name.

The original meaning for the word. 'defend' that is used in our passage is "set you on a high place". This implies that the name of the Lord "sets you on high place". That's where you have been placed by God in Christ. The high place is your place. Glory!

Beloved, for you to be set on high place with full defence, you need to embrace the name of Jesus Christ and exercise your faith in that defending and defenceful name.

(f) THE NAME THAT GUARANTEES INFALLIBILITY

***Some trust in Chariots, and some in horses; but we will remember the name of the LORD our God. They are brought down and fallen; but we are risen, and stand upright.* (Psalms 20:7, 8)**

The name of our Lord Jesus Christ is the only name given to us that guarantees our standing upright and to be infallible. As such, absolute trust and strong faith exercised in the name is required for our infallibility. While those who trust in other strength and source of power are brought down and fallen, we shall rise up and stand uprightly.

(g) THE NAME TO PUSH DOWN OUR ENEMIES AND TREAD UNDER ALL THAT RISE UP AGAINST US

***Through thee will we push down our enemies, through thy name we will tread them under that rise up against us.* (Psalm 44:5)**

The guarantee that every true son and daughter of God has for victory is that through God shall we push down our enemies, and through the name of Jesus Christ shall we tread under, all that rise up against us.

Beloved, by the supreme name of Jesus Christ at the disposal of the body of Christ, that is, God's people, none among true believers should be under the enemies' insurgence. It becomes an aberration. Rather, every one of us should operate above them – the Devil and all the powers of darkness in victory. We are to push them down through God who fights our battles for us and through the name of Jesus shall we tread down everyone who rises up against us (Exo. 14:14).

(h) THE NAME – A DELIVERER IN TIME OF TROUBLE

> ***Call upon me in the day of trouble: I will deliver thee, and thou shalt glorify me.*** **(Psm 50:15)**

Beloved, the Lord Jesus Christ and the power in His name guarantees our deliverance from trouble and in the time of trouble. All you need to do is to trust absolutely in that name and make it your confession, and then you will enjoy the great deliverance that the name brings.

> ***Surely shall one say, in the LORD have I righteousness and strength: even to him shall men come; and all that are incensed against him shall be ashamed.*** **(Isaiah 45:24)**

TESTIMONY, USING HIS NAME IN THE FACE OF DANGER

Sometime in the year 2014, by the revelation of the Holy Spirit, I was led o a spot in front of the main auditorium of our Mission Church, Triumphant Faith Missions Interna-tional, Elebo Village [God's Wonders' Prayer Ground], Olorunda-Abaa, Ibadan, where a Muslim Cleric – Alfa and his witch wife had dug a small pot (oru in Yorubaland) having some fetish substances in it and buried the charm under the ground. We however dug it out. Suddenly, immediately thereafter, a swarm of visible bees was sent to attack me with a view to stinging me to death. The swarm of bees filled thy sky and came toward me.

Having understood the evil intention of the wicked by discernment of the spirit and manifestation of word of knowledge, I asked the two young men who were with me outside the auditorium to go inside, and I bound the spirit behind the bees' attack and declared them to go back to the sender, by making use of the name of Jesus Christ. To the glory of God, the swarm of bees that filled the atmosphere disappeared immediately. The name of Jesus Christ is indeed a deliverer in the day of trouble and from all troubles and from those that trouble you.

(i) THE NAME FOR JUSTIFICATION

> ***In the Lord shall all the seed of Israel be justified, and shall glory.* (Isaiah 45:25)**

The Lord Jesus and power in His name are our justifiers. Faith in Him and in His name is what guarantees us for justification from every condemnation of the Devil.

> ***Therefore, being justified by faith, we have peace with God through our Lord Jesus Christ.* (Rom. 5:1)**

Beloved, if we keep giving account of the greatness of the name of Jesus Christ, no volume of any book in this world can be able to contain it. It suffices to say that immeasurable, unquantifiable, unfathomable and inexplica-ble is the power inherent in the name of Jesus Christ. It is also by Him and by His name that we have access by faith into this grace (super power of God that we are endowed with, which enables us to do what is naturally impossible) (Rom. 5:2)

Conclusively, the name of Jesus Christ is efficacious in handling any issue of life for the victory of anyone who exercises his or her faith in the name, over the Devil Halleluyah!

> ***Our help is in the name of the LORD, who made the heaven and earth.* (Psm. 124:8)**

CHAPTER 8

The Word of God for Victory Over the Devil

One sure weapon which can never fail to guarantee our maintenance of our God-given victory over the Devil, through our Lord Jesus Christ is the word of God. This word is Jesus. The potency of Jesus and everything that Jesus Christ represents is in the word of God. As such, the word of God, which is the word of His power, is an arsenal that the Devil cannot withstand, when it is rightly used.

In the book of Luke, Chapter 4 and verse 4, we saw that the only weapon that our Lord Jesus Christ made use of during His trial by the Devil, while on earth was the word of God. This word of God, which is the word of His testimony, is a weapon of our victory, and it enhances the maintenance of the victory, above the Devil and all powers of darkness.

The efficacy of the word of God as a weapon against the Devil in victory is multidimensional. Is it in healing? He sent His word and healeth them and delivers them from all their destructions. Is it in power? The word of God is the word of His power. In salvation, it is the word of salvation; it is the Gospel of Christ, which is the power of God unto salvation.

Also, the word works wonders. The word can never die, it can never fail, it can never fall. It is **inerrant**. The heaven and earth shall pass away, but not a jot of God's word shall pass away without being fulfilled. For ever, the word of God is settled in heaven. Psalm 119:89; Matthew 5:18; 24:35.

However, for the word to work for you in the demonstration of Jesus' victory over the Devil, you will need to do the following with it:

1. Embrace the word – Psm. 19:7,8, 10; 119:105
2. Magnify the word of God as God Himself has highly exalted it above all His names – Ps 138:2
3. Study the word – 2 Tim. 2:15
4. Search the scriptures – John 5:39
5. Let the word richly dwell in you – Col 3:16
6. Bear it in your heart, to be mixed with faith in you. Prov. 4:21; Heb 4:2; Job 22:22
7. Meditate in the word – Joshua 1:8; Psm. 119:148, 97
8. Profess the word – Rom. 10:8,9
9. Put the word into action. Apply the word and be a doer of the word – James 1:22-25
10. Preach the word in season and out of season – 2 Tim. 4:2
11. Teach the word – Matt. 28:18
12. Pray the word – John 15:7; 1 John 5:14
13. Wait for the Lord and hope in His word – Ps. 130:5
14. Receive Direction by the word – Ps. 119:105
15. Get understanding by the word – Psm. 119:104
16. Get illumination (light) by the word – Psn, 119:130; 19:8b
17. Walk in the light of the word – John 8:12
18. Get empowered by the word – Eccl 8:4
19. Think the word and make it the imagination of your heated life – Prov. 23:7; 2 Cor. 10:4
20. Let the word be the principle of your life – Psm. 119:105
21. Receive healing and deliverance from destruction by the word – Psm. 107:20
22. Guard or secure your heart with God's word for issues of life to be your portion.

23. Acquaint yourself with God by the word, so that you can have peace – Job 22:21.
24. Have a change of life, character, attitude, behavioural pattern by the word of God – Psm. 19:7
25. Be rejoiceful by the word – Psm. 19:18a.

CHAPTER 9

Prayer

Prayer is another strong unbeatable spiritual weapon that God has committed into the hands and lives of believers in order for us to maintain the top in victory.

Prayer is a spiritual exercise. In prayer your spirit is contacting the Father-God, who is Spirit. Sense knowledge cannot grasp this. Its operation is in the realm of the recreated spirit. It is regenerated spirit of man, contacting and conversing with the Almighty God.

What exactly is prayer? Prayer has been defined as a-2 way communication between God and man. In a better note, **prayer is communication from a mortal man to an Immortal God for His ready interven-tion.**

This Author defined Prayer in his mimeograph titled: ***Quiet Time*** as an expression and manifestation of our faith in God, because whosoever comes to God must believe that he is and that he is a rewarder of them that diligently seek Him (Heb. 11:5).

Prayer is an open cheque given to man by God to cash from His unlimited heavenly resources. Our Lord Jesus Christ said in the Gospel of Matthew chapter 7 verses 7 and 8 thus:

> ***Ask, and it shall be given you, seek, and ye shall find: knock, and it shall be opened unto you: For every one that asketh receiveth; and he that seeketh findeth; and to him that knocketh it shall be opened.***

Amplified version of the bible put the passage above thus:

> ***Keep on asking and it will be given you; keep on seeking and you will find; keep on knocking (revently) and the door***

> ***will be opened to you. For every one who keeps on asking receives, and he who keeps on seeking finds and to him who keeps on knocking it will be opened.***

Prayer is a continuous spiritual exercise which a Christian engages in as long as he or she puts on this mortal flesh.

Also, prayer is said to be a spiritual exercise at man's disposal which moves the hands that created the heavens and earth to his own advantage and to the glory of God.

The implication of this last definition given to prayer is that by that spiritual exercise or weapon of prayer, there is nothing you cannot achieve. Yes! You are to make anything happen in your community, city, nation and throughout the world, by the instrumentality of prayer, by which you exercise and manifest your God-given dominion – Gen. 1:26-28; Psm. 2:8.

PRAYER OF FAITH

However, for prayer to God to work for you in absolute manifestations of victory, it must be prayer of faith.

What is prayer of faith? It is prayer that is said with absolute trust and confidence in the Most High God to achieve all things.

> ***. . . Without faith, it is impossible to please him; for he that cometh to God must believe that he is, and that he is a rewarder of them that diligently seek him.*** **(Heb. 11:6)**

Amplified version of the bible put the passage above thus:

> ***But without faith, it is impossible to please and be satisfactory to Him. For whosoever would come near to God must (necessarily) believe that God exists and that He is the Rewarder of those who earnestly and diligently seek Him (out).***

- Prayer of faith is prayer that dwells in possibilities, as against impossibilities.
- Prayer of faith is prayer that is said according to the will of God which is bound to be answered (1 John 5:14).
- Prayer of faith is a Mountain moving prayer (Mark 11:23; Isaiah 54:10).
- Prayer of faith is prayer of Miracles (James 5:14-15).
- Prayer of faith is prayer of focus that focuses on the Almightiness of God alone. It is a die hard minded prayer said to God without drawing back until result is achieved by it (Heb. 10:39).
- Prayer of faith is prayer of blessings (Jer. 17:5-8).
- Prayer of faith is central to Christian living (Heb. 10:38).
- Prayer of faith is prayer of operation and demonstration of deliverance from every affliction of the Devil (James 5:13; Psalm 50:15; Jer. 29:12-14).

This kind of prayer – prayer of faith is what God requires from us. It is the ever availing prayer. It is the pattern that our Lord Jesus Christ laid down for us to follow.

When the Lord Jesus taught the Disciples on how to pray, He taught them this way: ***"Our father who art in heaven. Hallowed be thy name"*** **(Matthew 6:9)**.

It is worthy of note that our Lord's prayer was focused and directed to God alone and that God is "Our Father who is in heaven". Halleluyah! And He hallowed Him. The simple implication is that our prayers must be directed to God alone and it must be started by hallowing Him. Yes! by revering Him.

Prayer of faith was manifested by our Lord Jesus Christ in raising Lazarus from the grave (Read the account in John 11:1-5, 11-26, 33-45).

WHAT WE CAN AVAIL WITH PRAYER

Beloved, we can be so utterly ruled and governed by the word and by the Holy Spirit that we become Masters over demons and over their works. We cast out demons with the word, we pray for sick folks and diseases leave them; weakness is destroyed by the strength of God. The very life of God flows out through our lips.

I know that our prayers bring the very presence of God upon men in any part of the world. You see, this is cooperating with Him. God through you is ruling the demons and evil forces all over the world. You become His voice in that name. The word really becomes the sword of the spirit, and it is waging war against demonic forces who rule men. His word through your lips dominates these world forces. They don't know it, but they feel cramped, bound, hindered, conquered.

Jesus said, "In my name, ye shall cast out demons". That means rule over them, govern them. God through you then can sway the nations.

Now, you can understand 2 Corinthians 6:1 ***"Laboring together with Him"***.

How? Through this marvellous prayer life. You have entered the Holy Priesthood in your prayer life. You can be God's voice, His spoke man or spoke woman, His Ambassador, His under ruler in Jesus' Name through the word in your lips. You are taking Jesus' place. You are acting in His stead – Once more, God is set free among man.

You remember that God gave to Adam dominion over the entire universe. That dominion was restored to us through Jesus, but it is of no value to us, unless we the Jesus' men use that authority in His name. That was given to an individual, Adam; Now the authority is given to us as believers in His name.

Jesus exercised that dominion. He ruled the sea, He ruled the fish. He ruled the human body. He made legs grow where they had been amputated. He fed the multitudes.

We are surrounded by demonic forces that are dominating the human on earth and the Church has authority over them. Prayer is our method and mode of dominating these diabolical forces that are wrecking civilization.

YOU HAVE A PLACE IN THE PRAYER LIFE

It is imperative to say that every one of us as believers has a place in the prayer life. God has no unused members. There is no useless member in the physical body, neither is there in the spiritual body of Christ.

God has planned with divine wisdom, the body of Christ and the moment that you are born into that body, you have your place in which to function. If anyone thinks that because of lack of training or for lack of this or that, he hasn't a place, he is deluded by the enemy. You have a place

With that place comes responsibility and with responsibility comes a reward or demerit.

Beloved, if you do not take your place in the family of God, in the church and begin to function, the body of Christ is weakened because of it.

Some have the idea that their special vocation is to criticize others because they are not doing more. The Holy Spirit is the only one who has this position. You have no right to set yourself up as a critic. Your business is to find your place and fill it. Until you do, you will pay the price. I want you to know, my brother, my sister, that the price you pay for staying out of the will of God is expensive. You may pay it in sickness, in loss of money or in unhappiness with your loved ones, for you cannot be the protected one, the cared- for one as long as you are standing outside of the Lord's will for you.

Take your place! Give yourself to meditation, prayer and study of the word. Don't allow anything to stand in the way of your finding your place.

Life will not mean much to you outside of His will. The big thing of life is to be in the Will of the Father.

Perhaps, your saying is that you were never called to give your life in prayer? No, you may not have been set apart by the spirit for that special ministry, but I think it would be wise for you to spend enough time in prayer to get acquainted with the Father (Luke 18:1).

There are only two ways of getting acquainted with the Father: through the word, and by prayer.

If you don't take time to pray, you are losing out. You can't say that you have no responsibility in the prayer life, for you have. To run away from the greatest duty of prayer that you can offer to God for yourself, your family and others is to accept defeat of yourself, your family and others before Satan, whom Jesus Christ had defeated.

Beloved, you must go back to your prayer closet and begin your new fellowship with God. It is by this you will be able to demonstrate your victory through our Lord Jesus Christ over the Devil.

WHY YOU MUST PRAY

Numerous are reasons ascribed to why you must pray. The following are few among them.

1st: Our God is a prayer answering God

> ***PRAISE waiteth for thee, O God, in Sion, and unto thee shall the vow be performed O thou that hearest prayer . . . .* (Psalm 65:1-2a)**

2nd: All flesh that want their prayers to be answered must of necessity come to God.

> ***O thou that hearest prayer, unto you shall all flesh come.* (Psalm 65:2)**

3rd God has chosen you and caused you to approach Him with a view to relating with Him through the instrumentality of prayer, in order for you to be blessed and be satisfied with the goodness of His house and holy temple.

> ***Blessed – happy, fortunate (to be envied) – is the man whom you choose and cause to come near, that he may dwell in your Courts! We shall be satisfied with the goodness of your House, Your Holy Temple.* (Psalms 65:4, Amplified Bible)**

Beloved, God has chosen you as His beloved son or daughter by election of grace through our Lord and Saviour Jesus Christ. By that privilege, He has caused you to be intimated or be in fellowship with Him, so that you may live, maintaining His presence through the instrumentality of prayer, in order for you to be satisfied with the goodness of His House, even of His Holy Temple. Many blessings are lost by God's people who fail to take everything to Him in prayer.

4th Prayer is the major medium through which you will allow God to act terribly in righteousness for your sake.

By fearful and glorious things (that terrify the wicked, but make the godly sing praises) do you answer us in righteousness - rightness and justice - O God of our salvation. You who are the confidence and hope of all the ends of the earth, and of those far off on the seas. (Psalm 65:5)

Beloved, prayer is the spiritual force by which God shall terribly act on your behalf in your favour, against the wicked.

5th Prayer is also an avenue to receive help from the Lord who made the heaven and the earth from whom our help comes. Psm. 121:1-2

6th Prayer is the force that enables you to become the best that God wants you to be, relying absolutely in His strength – 1 Sam. 2:9

7th To invoke God's destructive intervention upon your adversaries and adversaries of the Lord – 1 Sam. 2:10

8th For you to put the Devil where he belongs – James 4:7

9th For you to possess people and the earth for God and as your inheritance – Psalm 2:8

10thFor direction – Psalm 37:23-24

11thFor the salvation of the Lord – Psalm 37:39-40

12thFor you to endure in the faith unto the end and inherit God's kingdom – Heb. 10:30

13thTo have evil removed and reversed from our lives and destiny by God's intervention – Psalm 50:15.

14thFor God to recompense tribulation to them that trouble you – 2 Thess 1:6

15thFor you to fulfil destiny.

16thFor daily and lasting relationship with the Father.

17thBy it, your faith in God is kept alive.

18thFor you to see the mighty hands of God at work in your favour.

19thFor you to see the end of your enemy and trouble.

20thFor you to rule your world – Psm. 2:8.

CHAPTER 10

Fasting

Fasting is another spiritual exercise that is spiritually prescribed which enables man to put flesh – carnality and soul – soulicality into subjection in order for the spirit in him to be alive and dominate. Fasting as a spiritual exercise goes side by side with prayer. Reason is that any fasting-exercise that a person engages in without prayer is nothing but hunger strike. What then is fasting?

Fasting is simply abstinence from what the flesh desires, such as food, drink, etc. with a view to killing the flesh so that the spirit can be alive. In addition to prayer, fasting is an effective spiritual weapon to be used in effecting deliverance in every facet of human endeavours, be it spiritual, physical, emotional, social, financial, and material and what have you.

The efficacy of ***fasting*** as a weapon in effecting deliverance cannot be overemphasized. The inevitability and importance of this weapon made our Lord and Master, Jesus Christ to prescribe it for anyone who desires some peculiar deliverance. In other words, prayer that is backed up with fasting is a sure weapon to enhance deliverance for mankind from even the most dreaded satanic bondage. This efficacy of the weapon – ***'fasting'*** was graphically demonstrated in the Deliverance Ministry of our Lord Jesus Christ, whilst He was on earth as seen in the following scriptural passage:

> ***. . . when they were come to the multitude, there came to him a certain man kneeling down to him, and saying Lord have mercy on my son: for he is lunatic, and sore vexed: for oftentimes he falleth into the fire, and oft into the water. And I brought him to thy disciples and they could not cure***

him. And Jesus rebuked the devil; and he departed out of him: and the child was cured from that very hour. Then came the disciples to Jesus apart, and said why could not we cast him out? And Jesus said unto them, because of your unbelief; for verily I say unto you, if ye have faith as a grain of mustard seed, ye shall say unto this mountain, remove hence to yonder place; and it shall remove; and nothing shall be impossible unto you. Howbeit this kind goeth not out but by prayer and fasting. (Matthew 17:14-21)

Beloved reader, do you yearn for personal deliverance, community deliverance, deliverance for a nation, in a business, in a home or in any area? All you need is: by faith in the God of Deliverance, add to your prayer, fasting and ***great deliverance*** which Almighty God effects in lives of people who come unto Him shall be yours (Psalm 50:15).

In fact, the motive behind every fasting as a spiritual exercise that God's people (you) engage in should be liberation or deliverance from the bands of wickedness. Hence, the Almighty God said:

Is not this the fast that I have chosen? To loose the bands of wickedness, to undo the heavy burdens, and to let the oppressed go free and that ye break every yoke. (Isaiah 58:6)

Dear reader, this is your moment of absolute freedom from every band of wickedness that is over your life, home business, destiny and over your loved ones, as you endeavour to take advantage of this spiritual weapon, called fasting to loose the band of wickedness, undo satanic heavy burdens and declare your freedom from the oppression and yokes of the wicked.

I therefore, declare you free from every bondage, oppression, affliction, burden and yoke of the Devil, in Jesus' mighty name (Amen).

CHAPTER 11

Authority of the Believers

Jesus Christ, after His resurrection and before ascension declares:

> ***All power is given unto me in heaven and in earth.*** **(Matt. 28:19)**

This power is what He in turn gave to the believers with a commission to "go and teach all nations (make disciples of all nations)".

In another place, He declared:

> ***Behold, I give unto you power to tread on serpents and scorpions, and over all the power of the enemy: and nothing shall by any means hurt you.*** (Luke 10:**19)**

Unto every believer (you) is the power given, to subdue and live in dominion cum authority over all forces of darkness that have power to put people in bondage. In another place, Jesus said:

> ***These signs shall follow them that believe; In my name shall they cast out devils . . . They shall take up serpents, and if they drink any deadly things, it shall not hurt them; they shall lay hands on the sick, and they shall recover.*** **(Mark 16:17, 18)**

The aforementioned authority that rightly belongs to believers (you) for deliverance from forces that put people in bondage as revealed in the scriptures above is effective as enumerated below:

- To cast out demons in Jesus' name

- To take up serpents and drink deadly thing without being hurt
- To lay hands on them that are held bound by sickness and for them to be released and receive complete recovery or healing.

Nonetheless, Jesus declares again saying:

> ***Verily I say unto you, whatever ye shall bind (or diswant) on earth shall be bound (or diswanted) in heaven; and whatsoever ye shall loose (want) on earth shall be loosed (wanted) in heaven.*** **(Matt. 18:18)**

The above scriptural injunction is an addendum to the believers' authority to either let victims of bondage of believer be free from it, being endued with authority to loose and bind; want and diswant; The choice is now yours, to usurp the authority to your advantage for deliverance for yourself or and for others.

The potency of the authority conferred on believers is so great that God's guarantee on it is that no power, authority or opinion-making body in hell shall prevail against them.

> ***. . . Upon this rock (knowledge of Jesus Christ as the Son of the living God and the authority conferred by Him) I will build my church: and the gates of hell shall not prevail against it.*** **(Matt. 16:18)**

With all these authorities conferred on believers in Christ Jesus, we can issue decrees and declare judgement on the binding forces of darkness.

> ***Thou shalt . . . declare a thing, and it shall be established unto thee: and the light shall shine upon thy ways.*** **(JOB 22:28)**

> ***. . . Every tongue that shall rise against thee in judgement thou (You) shalt condemn. This is the heritage of the***

> ***servants of the LORD, and their righteousness is of me, saith the LORD.*** **(Isa. 54:17)**

In another place, it is written thus concerning you and against your enemies side by side:

> ***Take counsel together, and it shall come to nought but, you (God's child) shall speak the word, and it shall stand, for God is with us.*** **(Isa. 8:10)**

Gideon made use of the Authority and the sun stayed for a whole day in accordance with his directive which enhanced his victory and deliverance. God has made you to be greater than Gideon (Matt. 11:11). So, greater damage can be done to the kingdom of darkness through you, while much glorious works in deliverance can be done when you obediently make use of your authority as required and all glory shall be God's.

Beloved, it is your responsibility to make use of the authority which God has freely made yours by election of Grace. Therefore, I implore you to earnestly take advantage of the authorities to your deliverance, triumphant and blessed advantages.

CHAPTER 12

The Spirit and Power

The life and act of every believer whom God had won the battle over the Devil and all forces of darkness for through His only begotten Son – Jesus Christ should be such that demonstrates the Spirit and power of God. Paul in His Epistle to the Corinthians buttressed this truth when he wrote saying:

> ***And my speech and my preaching was not with enticing words of man's wisdom, but in demonstration of the spirit and of power.***
> **(1 Cor. 2:4)**

Amplified version of the Bible put the passage thus:

> ***And my language and my message were not set forth in persuasive (enticing and plausible) words of wisdom, but they were in demonstration of the (Holy) spirit and power (that is a proof by the spirit and power of God on me and stirring in the minds of my hearers the most holy emotions and thus persuading them).***

Beloved, our Lord Jesus Christ did all that He did in His earthly Ministry, because he was endued with power from on High, that is, the power of the Holy Spirit which He manifested and demonstrated. The records of these are in the Gospels and the Acts.

Our Lord Jesus Christ, after He was anointed with the Holy Spirit and power declaratively said:

> ***The spirit of the Lord is upon me, because he hath anointed me to preach the gospel to the poor. He hath sent me to heal the broken hearted, to preach deliverance to the captives, and recovering of sight to the blind, to set at liberty them that are bruise. To preach the acceptable year of the Lord.***
> **(Luke 4:18, 19)**

Also, it was recorded that by the anointing of the Holy Spirit and power, our Master Jesus Christ was equipped and made fit that He went about doing good and diverse miracles were performed by Him. This was done to demonstrate the supremacy of the power of God over the Devil and all his works, operations and actions that are poised to doing three principal evils: to steal, to kill and to destroy: Acts 10:38; John 10:10.

> ***How God anointed Jesus of Nazareth with the Holy Ghost and with power: who went about doing good, and healing all that were oppressed of the devil: for God was with Him.* (Acts 10:38)**

Also, going through the Calvary experience of being brutalised, crucified and died the death of the cross, it was only possible for Him to endure all these by the enable-ment of the Spirit and power.

Nevertheless, it did not stop at that. Our Master Jesus was buried in tomb, well guarded by security men of that time who were placed there by those who chose to crucify Him for no offence that He committed, but for the fulfilment of the scriptures about Him, which was unknown to them.

However, by the same Spirit and power, He went to hell, He delivered the saints who were bound there, got them resurrected. He also got the key of hell and of death from the Devil and resurrected from death the third day.

Beloved, all these were made possible for our Master Jesus Christ to bear in the flesh, but by the succour, comfort, energising, fortification and enablement of the Holy Spirit. The Good news is that our Lord Jesus Christ was crucified, shed His precious blood for the remission of the sins of the world, died, buried, but resurrected for our justification and finally, He ascended after He had shown Himself to His disciples and others, before whom He was taken up to heaven, seated right now, at the right hand of God the father, far above all principality, and power, and might, and dominion, and every name that is named, not only in this world, but also in that which is to come.

> ***Jesus, when he had cried again with a loud voice, yielded up the ghost. And behold, the veil of the temple was torn in two from the top to the bottom; and the earth did quake, and the*** 54 ***rocks were split; And the graves were opened; and many bodies of the saints that slept were raised. And came out of the graves after resurrection, and went into the holy city, and appeared unto many. Now, when the centurion and they that were with him watching Jesus, saw the earth-quake, and those things that were done, they feared greatly, saying, truly, this was the Son of God.*** **(Matt. 27:50-54)**

Beloved, the giving up of the ghost or death of our Lord Jesus Christ, His burial and resurrection caused a great disaster on your behalf and my behalf to the devil and the host of darkness. It caused great defeat to the graves, death and hell.

The saints that were asleep were resurrected and when our Lord Jesus Christ was buried, the grave could not host Him, Yes! The grave vomited Him; the death released the key into His hand. The Devil also being dealt with by our Master Jesus Christ released the keys in his hand. All obstacles and closed doors put in place by the forces of darkness were removed and forced open by the unfailing power of the Holy Spirit for our Lord to take over and the dominion which mankind had lost to Devil through Adam was restored to man by the Lord's death and resurrection, because the Lord resurrected and His resurrection is for the justification of mankind from all inherited condemnations caused by the sin of Adam.

Nevertheless, after our Lord resurrected, He ascended up to heaven, having disarmed principalities and powers on our behalf and made a public shame of them, triumphing over them in Him – (Col. 2:15).

Beloved, the effect of the triumph of Jesus on you and I is that we are triumphant in Him over the Devil and hosts of darkness. God had by it delivered us from the influence, authority and being under the powers of darkness and had translated or transferred us into the kingdom of His dear Son, at His right hand, far above all principalities and powers.

> ***Death is swallowed up in victory. O death, where is thy sting? O grave, where is thy victory? The sting of death is sin and the strength of sin is the law. But thanks be to God, who giveth us the victory through our Lord Jesus Christ.*** **(1 Cor. 15:54-57)**
>
> ***And having disarmed, spoiled principalities and powers, he made a show of them openly, triumphing over them in it.*** **(Col. 2:15)**
>
> ***Giving thanks unto the Father, who hath made us [fit] to be partakers of the inheritance of the saints, who hath delivered us from the power of darkness, and hath translated us into the kingdom of his dear son.***
>
> ***In whom we have redemption through his blood, even the forgiveness of sins. (Col. 1:12-14)***

Our Lord Jesus Christ declared:

> ***I am he that liveth, and was dead; and, behold, I am alive for evermore, Amen, and have the keys of hades (hell) and of death.*** **(Rev. 1:18)**

This victory of Jesus over all the host of darkness is on our behalf. Our victory is in the victory which He had won for us. Therefore, we are complete in Him and in His victory over the Devil. We are also made to be seated with Him in heaven, at the right of God the father. All these were made possible by the person, spirit and power of Holy Spirit.

> ***And hath raised us up together, and made us sit together in heavenly places in Christ Jesus.*** **(Eph. 2:6)**

> ***Far above all principality, and power, and might, and dominion, and every name that is named, not only in this world, but also in that which is to come.*** **(Eph. 1:21)**

Beloved, your victory over the Devil and his hosts of darkness had been settled by the Lord Jesus Christ. All that you need to do henceforth is to appropriate the victory and demonstrate the same over all principalities, and powers and dominion and every manifestation of darkness. To do this, you have to rely on the divine personality and power of the Holy Spirit. Yes! You have to be baptized with the Holy Spirit with the evidence of speaking with other tongues. (Mark 16:17; Acts 2:1-4).

Also, you have to be constantly and consistently filled with the Holy Spirit and power (Acts 1:4-5, 8; Joel 2:28-30).

Nevertheless, fellowship with the Holy Spirit, receive His anointing, retain the same and covet His continuous leading and refreshing – 2 Cor. 13:14; Acts 10:38.

Above all, be open to the Holy Spirit and give Him the right of way. By this, you'll ever remain over and above the Devil and powers of darkness and you will never be under them. Yes! You'll live your life always in victory over sin, the world and the Devil.

> ***For whatever is born of God overcometh the world; and this is the victory that overcometh the world, even our faith. Who is He that overcometh the world, but he that believeth that Jesus Christ is the son of God"*** **(1 John 5:4, 5)**

Dear reader, for you to be possessed of the Spirit of God and His power, you first need to become a child of God, by simply acknowledge that you are a sinner and that you cannot save yourself. Acknowledge Jesus Christ as your Saviour, confess your sins unto Him and invite Him into your life as your Lord and Saviour – 1 John 1:8-9; Rom. 10:9; Rev. 3:20.

The Spirit of God is only for God's children, those who have been saved (John 3:3-6; 1:12). The Holy Spirit is not the spirit of the world and He is not that which the world can receive.

> ***Now, we have received not the spirit of the world, but the spirit which is of God, that we might know the things that are freely given to us of God. Which things also we speak, not in the words which man's wisdom teacheth, but which the Holy Ghost teacheth; comparing spiritual things with spiritual.*** **(1 Cor. 2:12, 13)**

Beloved, with the above in view, be born of God. Yes, you must be born of spirit, because, it is only when you are born of the Spirit that you can understand the thing of the spirit and also be able to partake of the blessings of the spirit which include the Anointing and power of the Holy Spirit and you will begin to do things in the Spirit, such as praying in the Holy Ghost, casting out of demons by the Spirit, being led of the Spirit, doing miracles by the Spirit of God and living in the spirit.

I therefore welcome you to the world of the Triumphant in Christ Jesus, by the demonstration of the Spirit and power of God.

CHAPTER 13

Thanksgiving

Another spiritual exercise that every child of God should engage in, in order to maintain victorious stance upon and above the Devil is to give thanks to God in all things. Thanksgiving is our expression of gratitude to God for His doings and undoings in our favour and to His glory.

A man who does not give gratitude to God shall be granded. But when a man is thankful, he shall be fruitful and shall have his tank, full, and when he is grateful, God shall make him great.

Apart from the fact that thanksgiving is God's instruction and command to us, when we engage ourselves in that exercise, whatever good that we give thanks to God for shall be made physically manifested and multiplied in our lives.

Also, by engaging ourselves in giving thanks to God, we are testifying and declaring to the Devil and all hosts of darkness that God is the source of every good thing in our lives, because: ***"every good gift and every perfect gift is from above, and cometh down from the father of light with whom is no variableness, neither shadow of turning*** **(James 1:17).**

> ***And they overcame him by the blood of the Lamb and by the word of their testimony; and they loved not their lives unto the death.*** **(Rev. 12:11)**

Beloved, there are numerous reasons for which we must give thanks to the Lord, out of which the following are enumerated:

1. We give thanks to enter the gate of God – Psalm 100:4

2. We give thanks to God for growing in faith – 2 Thess. 1:3a
3. We give thanks to God for love of brethren towards each other 1 Thess. 1:3b
4. We give thanks to God in everything for this is the will of God in Christ Jesus concerning us – 1 Thess. 5:18; Eph. 5:20
5. We give thanks to God for preserving our lives from consumption by His mercy- Lamentation 3:21-23.
6. We give thanks to God, who gives us the victory through our Lord Jesus Christ – 1 Cor. 15:57, 2 Cor. 2:14.
7. We give thanks to God for He sits on the throne – Rev. 4:9
8. We give thanks to God as our offer of sacrifice – Amos 4:5
9. We give thanks to God in all our requests to Him, because without thanksgiving, they are not complete – Phil. 4:6
10. You and I are to continue ceaselessly in prayer, and watch in the same with thanksgiving – Col. 4:2
11. For Church or any structural dedication to God's glory, it should be done with the companies of them that give thanks. Yes it should be done with thanksgiving – Nehemiah 12:31
12. You are to give or supply to meeting Godly needs in the church with thanksgiving unto God – 2 Cor. 9:11-12.

Beloved, it is the duty of every triumphant saint to come before the presence of God with thanksgiving. Thanksgiving is the key that opens the gate into God's presence. Any prayer, sacrifice or what have you that is being done in God's presence must always be started with thanksgiving.

> ***Let us come before his presence with thanks giving and make a joyful noise unto Him with Psalm.*** **(Psalm 95:2)**
>
> ***For the LORD is a great God, and great King above all gods.*** **(Psalm 95:3)**

Beloved, we are to make thanksgiving our lifestyle because that is one of our eternal services that we are to render unto the Most High (Rev. 7:12).

Thanksgiving provokes the power of God to manifest in unprecedented miracles. Our Lord Jesus Christ by the Lazarus' tomb, on the fourth day that the latter had been buried, prayed thus.

> ***". . . Father, I thank thee that thou hast heard me.*** **(John 11:41)**

He continued by saying:

> ***And I know that thou hearest me always; but because of the people which stand by I said it, that they may believe that thou hast sent me.***
>
> ***And when he thus had spoken, he cried with a loud voice, Lazarus, come forth. (John 11:42-43)***
>
> *The result was:*
>
> ***And he that was dead came forth bound hand and foot with grave clothes; and his face was bound about with a napkin. Jesus saith unto them, Loose him and let him go.*** **(John 11:44)**

Beloved, there are diverse miracles performable through any believer who cultivates the habit of giving thanks to God, the Father of all grace, who makes manifests His wondrous works through us, His children who relate with him in faith.

CHAPTER 14

Praise

Praise is another force or spiritual exercise that keeps you lifted upon and above the devil in triumph, for God inhabits the praises of His people.

> ***But thou art holy, O thou that inhabitest the praises of Israel.*** **(Psalm 22:3)**

Beloved, wherever the spiritual exercise of praise is used, God is compulsorily present there in His glory, in His splendour and in His awesomeness: and when God is present, it is apparent that devil cannot be present there. This is why praise is one of the most significant and potent weapons for deliverance that is inevitable for us to make use of in spiritual warfare (a hold on the book tilted: ***"Supernatural weapons for Believers' Delive-rance"*** by the same author explicates more on this).

Examining the Efficacy of Praise

> ***Let the saints be joyful in glory: let them sing aloud upon their beds. Let the high PRAISES of God be in their mouth, and a two edged sword in their hand.*** **(Psm 149:5, 6)**

For what? You make use of your praises of God as follows:

1. To execute vengeance upon the heathen (the wicked) and punishments upon the people.
2. To bind their kings (the kings of the hosts of wicked) with chains and their nobles with fetters of iron.

3. To execute upon them the judgement written (Psm 149:7-9). Numerous are judgement written against the wicked in the scriptures. Through the instrumentality of praise. Yes! as you endeavour to praise God wholeheartedly, those punishment or judgement shall be executed upon your enemies on your behalf. Halleluyah!

The above passage reveals a number of deliverance cum triumphant works or effects of praise, when it is employed.

First: By praise, God's vengeance will be released upon the wicked and anti-God.
Second: Praise enforces divine punishments upon the wicked people and forces of wickedness and darkness.
Third: By praise, the kings of the wicked are bound with chain.
Fourth: By the efficacy of praise, God's judgement is executed upon the wicked.

Also, praise as a potent weapon or force in the hand of a believer triggers fulfilment of prophesies – 2 Chronicles 20:14-24.

Dear reader, all the above and more are what you can use the force or weapon of praise to effect, anywhere and at any time.

> ***This honour has all his saints. Praise ye the LORD.*** **(Psalm 149:0)**

Beloved, the honour is yours to achieve the above with spiritual exercise of praise. I therefore implore you to take an advantage of the spiritual exercise for your victory.

Our God is fearful in praises (Exo. 15:11). Praising Him arouses and attracts His anger and indignation of His judgment against and upon your enemies and upon those that hate you.

Praise is also a weapon or force for the miraculous to take place

Beloved, when you pray to God, His attention is drawn, but when you praise Him, He is bodily present to do and undo great and terrific things in your favour against the devil and the forces of darkness.

> ***"The adversaries of the LORD shall be broken to pieces, out of heaven shall he thunder upon them: the LORD shall judge the ends of the earth; and he shall give strength unto his kings and exalt the horn of his anointed" (I Sam. 2:10).***

CHAPTER 15

Obedience

Obedience in this context is simply complying with God's words as instructed in the Holy Bible. It is doing the will of our heavenly father. It is taking on the inside God's word hook-line-and-sinker; and acting on same without subjecting it to human analysis or explanation.

It takes obedience to God for anybody to be fit for God's use and as a weapon for His deliverance against the enemy's operation.

Without obedience to God, Devil or demons will not be subject to man, because it is only by the fulfilment of our own allegiance to God can demon see us, tremble, and obey our command without ado.

> ***And having in readiness to revenge all disobedience, when your obedience is fulfilled (2 Cor. 10:6).***

It was this understanding of God's deliverance and blessings which come through obedience that Moses had which made him say to the people of God whom he was leading thus:

> ***See, I have set before thee this day life and good and death and evil; in that I command thee this day to love the LORD thy God, to walk in his ways, and to keep His commandments and his statutes and his judgements that thou mayest multiply: and the LORD thy God shall bless thee in the land wither thou goest to possess it. But if thine heart turn away, so that thou will not hear, but shalt be drawn away and worship other gods, and serve them: I denounce unto you this day that ye shall surely perish . . .*** **(Deut. 30:15-19).**

My prayer is that you will not perish, but rather live to prosper, because you will love your God, obey Him and you will not depart from worshipping Him.

Also, our Lord Jesus Christ emphasised the weapon of obedience which is an indication of a man's love for Him as a condition precedent to HIS LORDSHIP's love and manifestation to such a fellow.

> ***He that hath my commandments and keepeth them, he it is that loveth me: and he that loveth me shall be loved of my Father, and I will love him and will manifest myself to him.* (John 14:21)**

From the scriptural passage above, it is crystally clear that act of obedience to God's words, which is an indication of our (your) love for God is what guarantees God's love for us (you) in spite of the enemy's hatred and wicked acts. It (obedience) is also the singular weapon that guarantees the manifestation of the LORD's awesome power and glory favourably in your direction and against the wicked forces and their acts of wickedness.

Reader, there is power in obedience, Yes! there is blessing in it and of course, there is great victorious deliverance in obeying God. Therefore, I implore you by the mercy of God that you make obedience to Him your watch-word in this life's voyage. The resultant effect is that you will swim in the ocean of God's prosperity and deliverance, and your years on earth shall be a testimony of His glorious pleasure.

CHAPTER 16

Service

The word service in our context means "Duty or work done for God". It is a helpful act. In serving God, Jesus replied: ***No one who puts his hand to the plow (beings to serve) and looks back [wishing to go back to whatever he was doing before] is not fit for the service in the kingdom of God*** **(Luke 9:62).**

Beloved, service to God is one inevitable spiritual exercise or force that we must engage in as God's people for us to maintain the top position of victory over the Devil, principalities, powers, dominion and of course, over every situation and circumstances in the present and in future. You and I must have a work, a duty or a helpful act that we render ceaselessly, tirelessly, perseveringly and enduringly for God in this world unto the end without looking back. When you engage in service for God, He will bless your bread and water, He shall not allow you to cast out your young or be barren, He shall take away your sicknesses and diseases and make you fulfil your days in the land of the living.

> ***And ye shall serve the LORD your God, and he shall bless thy bread and thy water and He will take sickness away from the midst of thee. There shall nothing cast their young nor be barren in thy land: the number of thy days I will fulfil.*** **(Exodus 23:25-26)**

Beloved, service unto God includes rendering obedience and worship to God. Our Master Jesus said: ***"It is written, worship the Lord your God, and serve him only"*** **(Matthew 4:10).**

Also, when serving God, you should serve Him with gladness, not by cohesion, constraint or for eye service.

> ***Serve the Lord with gladness.*** **(Psm 100:2)**

Serving God also involves serving one another in love as God's children.

> ***Serve one another in love.*** **(Gal. 5:13)**

Dearest reader, if you obey and serve God, He will be an enemy to your enemies and an adversary to your adversaries; and shall send His Angel to go before you to bring you to all that are your enemies and haters and he shall cut them off.

> ***But if thou shalt obey His voice and do all that I speak, then I will be an enemy unto thine enemies; and an adversary unto thine adversaries. For mine Angel shall go before thee and bring thee in unto the Amorites, and the Hitites, and Perizites, and the Cananites, the Hivites and the Jebusites; and I will cut them off.*** **(Exodus 23:22-23)**

Also by serving God, He will send His Angel before you to keep you, guard you and secure you in the way and to bring you into your God-given place of destiny.

> ***Behold, I will send an Angel before thee to keep thee in the way and to bring thee into the place which I have prepared.*** **(Exo. 23:20)**

Beloved, God has a glorious destiny for you. Yes! He has a sure place of honour, dignity and fulfilment which He has prepared for you. It requires serving Him obediently for you to enjoy this unprecedented security to get there.

> ***He will keep the feet of his saints and the wicked shall be silent in darkness for by strength shall no man prevail.*** **(1 Samuel 2:9)**

Nevertheless, service will incur God's wrath upon your enemies and adversaries.

I will send hornets before thee, which shall drive out the Hivite, the Canaanite and the Hittite from before thee. (Exo. 23:28)

The adversaries of the LORD shall be broken to pieces; out of heaven shall he thunder upon them: the LORD shall judge the ends of the earth: and he shall give strength unto his king, and exalt the horn of his anointed. (1 Sam. 2:10)

Beloved, do you want your adversaries who are invariably the adversaries of the Lord to be broken to pieces and for God to thunder upon them from heaven? Yes! Do you want God's judgement upon your enemies and anti-Christ all over the world? Do you want God to strengthen you and exalt you? The simple answer to all these questions is; **serve God**.

Service is indeed God's great weapon in the hand of any man to attract deliverance from God, because He-God created man simply for His service (pleasure) – Rev. 4:11

Serving God is a guarantee to sure blessing, pleasurable living and victorious deliverance always.

If they . . . serve him (God), they shall spend their years in pleasures. (Job 36:11)

What is required of you for your absolute breakthrough is your service unto God. Serve Him with what you are, what you have and what you expect to be. Make Him the pivot (centre) of your life, home, business and all your endeavours. With absolute humility, serve the Lord.

When you do this, the light of His glory shall shine on you and all darkness and dark works of the workers of darkness will disappear and you will have testimony. So shall it be, in Jesus Mighty Name (Amen).

Jesus said:

> *The light of the body is the eye, if therefore thine eye be single, thy whole body shall be full of light. But if thine eye be evil, thy whole body shall be full of darkness . . . No man can serve two masters: for either he will hate the one, and love the other; or else he will hold to the one, and despise the other. Ye cannot serve God and mammon.* (Matt. 6:22-24)

My admonition to you is that you should set your gaze on God alone, via His word; and your transformation, restoration, life of emancipation and total victory shall be guaranteed.

> *. . . We all, with open face beholding as in a glass (of God's word) the glory of the LORD, are changed (transformed, recreated and lifted) into the same image from glory to glory (might to might, victory to victory and breakthrough to breakthrough) even so as by the spirit of the Lord (2 Cor. 3:18) [Sam O. Jimson's Edition]*

He – the Lord is the only one worthy to be looked upon and served.

> *They looked unto him, and were lightened (radiant) and their faces were not ashamed.* (Psm 3:5)

Other books by this Author are:

(1) Supernatural Weapons for Believer's Deliverance

(2) Breaking The Evil Blood Covenant

(3) Victory In Your Zero Hour

(4) Quiet Time: What, When, With Whom, Why and How?

(5) Way Out of Confusion

(6) Prayer Pattern For Conquest

(7) Living Word For Total Life

(8) Freedom For The Divorced

(9) Prayer Pattern For Conquest

(10) Golden Tips For Wealth and Riches

(11) From Spiritual Baby (Convert) Unto Spiritual Maturity (Gianthood)

(12) Prayer Compass For Victory

(13) Akoko Idakeje

(14) Destroying Curses

(15) Personal Deliverance Made Easy

(16) God Shall Arise

(17) Duty/Challenge To Pray With Biblical Types of Prayer

(18) Love God, Not Money, To Make Money

(19) Wait on God Till Your Change Comes

(20) Living Righteous Made Easy

www.ingramcontent.com/pod-product-compliance
Lightning Source LLC
LaVergne TN
LVHW052052160826
845678LV00015B/3194

* 9 7 9 8 8 4 6 4 3 9 0 9 2 *